For the Faint of Heart

Hope for the Hurting

By

Craig Parrott

XULON PRESS

Dedicated to Andrew, Rachel, and Mark

Whatever comes your way in life, may you always be drawn closer to our Heavenly Father, cast all your cares on Him, and know that He cares very much about you.

Love, Dad

Table of Contents

‮⚙‬

Acknowledgments

"With many counselors plans succeed" Proverbs 15:22 tells us. I have had many counselors collaborating with me on the words that follow. I am indebted to the many proofreaders who loved enough to speak the truth to me. Like David's Nathan, they knew I needed truth more than empty praises or false reassurances. Such friendships are precious and rare.

I wish to thank the many students, colleagues, and friends throughout the past twenty-three years who honored me by sharing their holy moments of pain. I have learned more than I have taught; I have been more encouraged than I have encouraged.

I wish to thank Cathy Hellmers, who graciously consented to proofreading one final time.

I wish to thank those who read with both head and heart and whose own lives have been punctuated by seasons of faint hearts. I value their honesty, their wisdom, and their faith. Among them are Nancy Duensing, Mark Hollenbeck, and Ron Brandhorst.

I wish to thank Dr. Andrew Spitznas, a former student and now dear friend, for his expertise and discernment walking by the Spirit in the field of psychiatry. I also admire his bold transparency.

I wish to thank Dr. Russ Moulds, Rev. David Ahlman, and Rev. Dwight Hellmers for their biblical insights and textual scrutiny. Their encouragement for me to pursue this project has been appreciated. More importantly, their being brothers in my times of adversity will undoubtedly provide them with jewels in their crowns in our heavenly home.

I wish to thank Tom Board for showing me God's Truth. My mind is still being transformed as I think about God's Words as spoken through him.

I wish to thank the authors found in the bibliography. God has touched me through them. Far from wishing to plagiarize, I hope this book draws new readers to them and to their writings.

I wish to thank my relatives—especially daughter Rachel, son Andrew, my mother, aunt Marlis, uncle Alan, and sister-in-law Erica—as they modeled for me grace and courage and faith when their hearts were faint.

I wish to thank my wife Rebecca whose own walk in trials makes her very beautiful in my eyes. Her encouraging words, publishing expertise, and countless hours fueled what you are now holding in your hands. This book is definitely the result of our partnership in the Gospel from the first day until now.

Most importantly, I wish to thank our great and gracious Heavenly Father. "I remember my affliction and my wandering, the bitterness and the gall. I well remember them, and my soul is downcast within me. Yet this I call to mind and therefore I have hope: Because of the Lord's great love we are not consumed, for his compassions never fail. They are new every morning; great is your faithfulness. I say to myself, 'The Lord is my portion; therefore I will wait for him.'" (Lam. 3:19–24) To Him be the glory.

Preface

This book uses a letter format with several aims in mind. First, it is hoped that a conversational tone, much like two friends might use over lunch or on a patio, might be gained. Second, it was my intention to keep each chapter fairly short and readable in one sitting.

"Michelle" is obviously a compilation of many names and faces over the years, including my own. Many people could probably read this book and recognize themselves in it but any resemblance to any one individual is certainly not by design. It might serve the reader to insert his or her own name when the name "Michelle" is read.

The original vision for this book was that pastors and congregational servants would have the book at their disposal and discretion to share with those around them undergoing various trials. The book could then become perhaps a devotional or inspirational reading. Others have suggested that they would use it for a Bible class; still others thought of small group use in homes. A few even thought of classroom use in Christian high schools and colleges. Much thought was given to including or excluding study questions for each chapter. Such material can be helpful, especially to lay leaders. I feared that such a section would give the book an academic flavor, rather than that of personal communication. I also felt that many such study guides give too much direction, direction that might not be suited for a particular audience. I finally concluded that readers could use those sections as they saw fit. Readers, therefore, are urged to use, rewrite, or ignore the questions for reflection and discussion that follow each chapter.

Little, if any, of the following material is original with this author. Bible references are cited and where possible so are quotes from other books. Again, I did not wish to disrupt the flow of conversation with footnotes. Luther quotes can be found in *What Luther Says* and in his fifty-plus volumes of writings.

Lastly, I fought against the temptation to give prescriptions and recipes. Bookstores are filled today with how-to manuals and step-by-step guides to overcoming this and that problem. I vigorously desired to avoid heaping more law onto already burdened hearts. It is hoped that hearts and minds will be redirected to God's promises and to His grace. His Word is what sustains us. His Word of truth is what sanctifies us. That is why God is given the last word in every letter.

A Personal Note

Dear Reader,

When I first realized that this book would become a reality, I wept. I suppose I cried for several reasons. First, it has been a lifelong dream of mine to write a book. Call it the English teacher in me. But, like so many down here, I thought dreams were just that—dreams. They never really come true. Ironically, my second reason for the tears was the sheer awesomeness of the task. Who am I to say anything to anyone about suffering? Bookstores are full of many excellent works on the topic. What can I say that is new? But I am now certain that the biggest reason that I cried was this: God is so good. Let me explain.

I vividly can recall on a moment's notice, and sometimes without any notice, lying on my back on my living room sofa. I am staring at the ceiling through watery clouds as hot tears burn my cheeks and stream down my face, tickling my ears. My crying in loud bursts suddenly slips into that silent scream, where the throat is gripped by the agony and all sound is quenched despite a gaping mouth. I am pleading, begging, and beseeching God to do something, anything with the pain I was feeling. I was asking Him over and over to make it all count, to make it all worth it, to redeem it somehow.

Since that experience, I have been blessed to see glimpses of how God has used the suffering in me to build greater perseverance, character, and hope. (Rom. 5:3–5) I have seen how He has chiseled away some of my rough edges and has polished more and more of my heart. I have seen how a few others have been touched by Him through me. And I am mindful of His Word in Ephesians 3:20–21: "Now to Him who is able to do immeasurably more than all we ask or imagine, according to His power that is at work within us, to Him be glory in the church and in Christ Jesus throughout all generations, for ever and ever! Amen."

I believe now that is the biggest reason that led me to weep. God is so good and His love endures forever. He really is able to do immeasurably more than all we ask or imagine. I did not dream on that tear-filled day that a book would result. And now here it is, in your hands. And, don't miss this part: God's power is at work within us. Perhaps especially when we don't feel as if it is.

It is my prayer that our God will use me and these words in this book to give you hope. I want to cheer you onward and upward as you run, and often walk or crawl, the race set before you. Ecclesiastes tells us there is nothing new under the sun. (Ecc. 1:9) You will not read anything new or revolutionary in this book. Many other authors have said what I will try to say. As Peter Kreeft has written, "We are all pygmies standing on the shoulders of giants." (*Making Sense Out of Suffering*) My "giants" are Larry Crabb and John Eldredge, Elisabeth Elliot and Peter Kreeft, Martin Luther and Augustine, Paul, Job, Jeremiah, David and, ultimately, Jesus. Perhaps these words will serve to point you in their direction. Perhaps you will see something for the first time in reading these words. Timing is crucial. I continue to have new revelations in reading Scriptures that I have read for years. Perhaps these words will do nothing for you … now. That is okay. Our times are in His hands. (Ps. 31:15) But be assured of a few things.

Wherever you are now, whatever has happened to you, whatever you have done, whatever you have failed to do, God is good and He is at work **within** you and He is at work **for** you. He is able to do immeasurably more than all you can possibly ask or imagine, even on your best day!

Martin Luther said that God does only two primary works in our lives: He breaks and He heals. You might feel extremely broken right now. Perhaps marital difficulties are burdening you. Perhaps a wayward or estranged child vexes you. Perhaps a doctor has delivered some frightening news about your health. Whatever has happened, your world has been turned upside down. Your mind roams between being dead in the water to being active and racing at all hours of the day, and usually more at night. I am writing to tell you that you have Hope. Weeping may last for the evening but joy is coming in the morning. (Ps. 30:5) We Believers are an Easter people and we believe in the resurrection of the dead. God is waiting to resurrect you. Because, you see, He is **for the faint of heart!**

Your fellow traveler being carried by His grace and precious promises,

Craig Parrott

January 2003

P.S.

"O Lord, do not rebuke me in your anger or discipline me in your wrath. Be merciful to me, Lord, for I am faint; O Lord, heal me, for my bones are in agony. My soul is in anguish. How long, O Lord, how long? Turn, O Lord, and deliver me; save me because of your unfailing love." (Psalm 6:1–4)

"You, O Lord, keep my lamp burning; my God turns my darkness into light." (Psalm 18:28)

"Be merciful to me, O Lord, for I am in distress; my eyes grow weak with sorrow, my soul and body with grief. My life is consumed by anguish and my years by groaning; my strength fails because of my affliction, and my bones grow weak ... But I trust in you, O Lord; I say, "You are

my God. My times are in your hands; deliver me
from my enemies." (Psalm 31:9–10, 14–15)

"O God, you are my God, earnestly I seek
you; my soul thirsts for you, my body longs for
you, in a dry and weary land where there is no
water." (Psalm 63:1)

"Who, O God, is like you? Though you have
made me see troubles, many and bitter, you will
restore my life again; from the depths of the
earth you will again bring me up. You will
increase my honor and comfort me once again."
(Psalm 71:19b–21)

"I cry aloud to the Lord; I lift up my voice to
the Lord for mercy. I pour out my complaint
before him; before him I tell my trouble. When
my spirit grows faint within me, it is you who
know my way." (Psalm 142:1–3)

"The Lord is faithful to all his promises and
loving toward all he has made. The Lord upholds
all those who fall and lifts up all who are bowed
down." (Psalm 145:13–14)

Letter One

"Why me, God?"

***

Dear Michelle,
I wonder if, "Why me, God?" might be the most frequently asked question of all time. It is probably no coincidence that many scholars believe the first book written in the Bible is Job. When we talk about universal themes, I think suffering just about covers it for everybody in all times and in all places. Jesus Himself told us, "In this world you will have trouble." (Jn. 16:33) We Christians are not exempt from it.

I realize that simply knowing this fact doesn't help much. I know that vegetables are good for me but that doesn't make them taste any better. And, when we are in the throes of a tough trial, it appears that the rest of the world is getting along smoothly. But appearances can be deceiving. It is important to realize that *everyone* undergoes troubles down here. *Everyone* struggles with some relationships at some point. *Everyone* battles circumstances that they can't control. And eventually *everyone* will face death.

Now I can hear your, "But what about so and so and what they have faced?" I admit, it seems that some people are called upon to endure more than others. I am not sure it is really fair or accurate to compare the trials of two different people. I mean, given their respective points of development, a high school break up can be just as traumatic to a teen as a divorce is to that teen's forty-something parents. But, for the sake of argument, let's say there are indeed some trials that are more difficult than others (and I believe there are!). Your question still stands, "Why me, God? What did I do to deserve this?"

Our old nature seems to have a penchant for demanding explanations to mysteries down here. That is, if we just discover the why's and how's, perhaps we can alter life and exert some degree of control over life's hurts and pains. We subconsciously, or even consciously, think we can limit or avoid some problems if we just find the map or formula of life. It is terrifying to consider that we might have very limited, if any, control over life. Such realization will lead us either to deep despair or to search with all our hearts for the One who is in control, or to both.

After Job's despairing and wishing he were never born, he sought out God. He wanted his day in court, so to speak, and he got it. And now you want your hearing. Brace yourself, Michelle; the following is not easy to hear, believe me! I don't pretend that it will be comforting on the first, second, or even tenth reading. But I think we are stuck with the same answer that Job received from Our Maker: "I will question you, and you shall answer me. Would you discredit My justice? Would you condemn Me to justify yourself?" (Job 40:7–8)

Do you see the attack on God's character in our very question? Who are You, God, to inflict this unhappiness on poor, innocent me? Such a question shows little understanding both of God's character and of ours! First, we are not innocent. We are deserving of death and hell due to our sinful nature. (Rom. 6:23) And second, God is God and we are not. We need to let that fact sink into our souls. God is the point—always. We are not. All of creation is made by and for and through Him. (Col. 1:15–17) We are a mist that appears for a little while and then vanishes. (James 4:14) We are dressed up dust and ashes.

Once this humbling realization takes hold of us, the question is moved into a different context, a context in which few people ever ask it. In times of prosperity and blessing, we might more justly ask, "God, why *me*?" Luther said, "If God were to take one of my eyes, break one of my legs, cause one of my arms to be lopped off, were to send me a sickness for eight days so that I could not work for a half year, what a crying and complaining would arise! At the same time, however, I would fail to remember that I have enjoyed hale and hearty days for fully twenty years. And though He were to take an eye, at least the other members are sound. Thus His punishments are not one-hundredth as great as the benefactions He bestows on us." So we see that, given the larger view of a lifetime, the vast majority of us enjoy infinitely more blessings than curses down here.

Perhaps the real question in times of trials and tribulations should be, "Why *not* me?" After all, troubles come to all humans and I am a mere human. If I were brutally honest with myself, I deserve much worse than whatever I am currently facing. My life has been filled with trillions of moments where I disobeyed, disrespected, and disbelieved the holy God of this universe. I should ask the question, "Why me, God?" whenever anything *good* enters my life!

But I believe this is only half the answer and a rather cold and raw one at that.

Jesus taught us to see God as our Father, or our "Daddy" to be more precise. To know God as a loving parent puts trials and troubles into a whole new light. To step outside ourselves and look at life from God's eternal perspective is eye opening. For one thing, what we consider to be "bad," might actually be "good." For example, when a parent spanks a child for crossing a dangerous street, to the child the incident is very bad. But to the parent who sees the greater reality, the incident is good in order to teach the child and provide for his well-being. In fact, for the parent to do nothing in such a setting would be very bad indeed and border on neglect.

Likewise, Hebrews encourages us to "endure hardship as discipline; God is treating you as sons" for "the Lord disciplines those He loves." (Hebrews 12:7, 6) Hardship trains us. "For what?" you ask. "That we may share in his holiness … it produces a harvest of righteousness and peace for those who have been trained by it." (Heb. 12:10–11)

One of the best New Testament answers to the question "Why?" is found in II Corinthians 1:8–9. Here the Apostle

Paul explains his sufferings like this: "We were under great pressure, far beyond our ability to endure, so that we despaired even of life. Indeed, in our hearts we felt the sentence of death. But this happened so that we might not rely on ourselves but on God, who raises the dead."

Is our loving Father using whatever crisis you are now facing to beg you to come running to His loving arms and jump into His lap? Is He allowing you to face more than you can handle so that you ask Him to handle it in His way for His glory and your good? Is He removing your trust in your health or finances or appearance or friends or family or intelligence so that you have nothing left but Him and His strength? Is He spotlighting you, like Job, in a grand spiritual battle in the heavenly places?

C.S. Lewis said it so well, "God whispers to us in our pleasures but shouts to us in our pains." Luther said, "When we enjoy peace and rest, we do not pray, we do not meditate on the Word but deal coldly with the Scriptures and everything that pertains to God." Think about it. Are you driven more closely to God's side during times of triumph or tragedy? If God alone is good, then anything that draws us closer to Him, even bad things, are ultimately used for our good. (Rom. 8:28)

But our loving and gracious Father doesn't stop there. He is training us not only to love Him, but also to love our neighbor: "Praise be to the God and Father of our Lord Jesus Christ, the Father of compassion and the God of all comfort, who comforts us in all our troubles, so that we can comfort those in any trouble with the comfort we ourselves have received from God." (II Cor. 1:3–4) Luther phrases it more elegantly than can I: "Thus God humbles His own in order to exalt them; He kills them in order to bring them back to life; He puts them to shame in order to glorify them; He casts them down in order to raise them up. God made Joseph lord of Egypt and master and savior of many people. How? By selling him, casting him off, and killing him. These are works of God which cannot be understood until they have been completed and finished."

Job never really received a direct answer from God to his question. But he learned that trust is more important than understanding in a relationship. He seemed to gain contentment by becoming silent and acknowledging that God was in control. There are many other choice places in Scripture that address this question, such as James 1 and Romans 5. The Psalms are filled with beautiful expressions of God's gracious work in our lives through seasons of suffering. We will explore some of these in later discussions. But for now, perhaps we can best sum up our answer this way: "Why me, God?"

"Be still, and know that I am God." (Psalm 46:10)

"'For My thoughts are not your thoughts, neither are your ways My ways,' declares the Lord. 'As the heavens are higher than the earth, so are My ways higher than your ways and My thoughts than your thoughts.'" (Isaiah 55:8–9)

"Oh, the depths of the riches of the wisdom

and knowledge of God! How unsearchable His judgments, and His paths beyond tracing out!" (Romans 11:33)

Learning to trust Him while not always understanding Him,

Craig

Chapter 1 Questions for Reflection and/or Discussion:

1. Have you ever asked, "Why me, God?" If so, what were your circumstances?

2. List your blessings that you have enjoyed throughout your life till now. Pause and thank God for them.

3. Looking over your life, when have you prayed most fervently to God?

4. It has been said that some of the most loving people have experienced suffering. Look at people in your life. Is this true?

What is the "good" God promises to work in all things?

᯽

"And we know that in all things God works for the good of those who love him, who have been called according to his purpose."

(Rom. 8:28)

Dear Michelle,
You really know how to ask the good, tough questions! I wish more people would ask this one. Unfortunately, many think they know the answer. And like many Bible verses, this one has been lifted out of context so often. People often look to material prosperity or improved health or a better relationship and think, "Aha, this is the "good" God has in mind for me." I think God's good goes much, much deeper.

Philosopher Peter Kreeft has written an excellent book on the subject. It is entitled *Making Sense Out of Suffering* and I highly recommend it. Several of his quotes come to mind that might be helpful for our discussion:

"What gives our lives meaning? Modernity answers "feeling good." The ancients answered "being good."

Sadly, our old, sinful nature strives at all costs — preventing us from trusting God and loving our neighbor — to feel good. Hence, we find people all around us trading one spouse for another, clinging to this or that addiction, distracting themselves with a cause, work, food, or sex. Whatever makes us feel good we define as "good." With such a view of "good," we will vainly try to control others and circumstances. God says through Isaiah, "Woe to those who call evil good and good evil. Woe to those who are wise in their own eyes and clever in their own sight." (Is. 5:20–21) I think it is safe to say that we don't know what is good for us! But fear not; we have One who does know what is good for us. Kreeft goes on to write:

"Now if soul is greater than body, then the good of the soul is greater than the good of the body ... What is the good of the body? Health, pleasure, freedom from suffering. What is the good of the soul? Wisdom and virtue..."

God seems to be far more interested in our character than in our circumstances, in our holiness than in our happiness. In Romans 5:3–4 we read, "suffering produces perseverance; perseverance character; and character hope." The Potter's hands mold and shape His children as they spin on the wheel of suffering. "In this you greatly rejoice, though now for a little while you may have had to suffer grief in all kinds of trials. These have come so that your faith—of greater worth than gold, which perishes even though refined by fire — may be proved genuine and may result in praise, glory, and honor when Jesus Christ is revealed." (I Pet. 1:6–7)

Philippians 1:6 tells us that God has begun a good work in us and He will bring it to completion when Jesus returns. The good that God seems to have in mind is our faith, hope, and love. In short, it is becoming Christlike, for whom and by whom the entire universe was created. And this is the context of Romans 8:28 as we see by reading verse 29: "For those God foreknew He also predestined to be conformed to the likeness of His Son, that He might be the firstborn among many brothers." Jesus is God's good plan; Jesus is the good; and God is so powerful and loving that He can and will use "all things" toward the end of forming us to become like Jesus. What greater good could God possibly do for us and in us?

According to Kreeft, "Sin has made us stupid so that we can only learn the hard way."

Luther put it this way: "One Christian who has been tried is worth a hundred who have not been tried, for the blessing of God grows in trials. He who has experienced them can teach, comfort, and advise many in bodily and spiritual matters." Again, we are back to loving God and the fruit that naturally follows, loving our neighbor. Perseverance, character, faith, hope, and love must be worthy pursuits for God to manifest in us. They certainly seem to be prerequisites to living a meaningful life down here. And they certainly won't come to us by our own effort to renounce suffering!

"The fruit of the Spirit is love, joy, peace, patience, kindness, goodness, faithfulness, gentleness and self-control." (Gal. 5:22–23) The Spirit seems to produce this fruit in the "furnace of affliction." (Is. 48:10) Jesus described the process of sanctification like this: "while every branch that does bear fruit He prunes so that it will be even more fruitful." (John 15:2) And pruning can be painful!

Have you ever noticed how seasoned gardeners work? Have you seen how they rise early in the morning, bend down low, and study their plants? They move slowly, gently brushing back leaves and stems so they can inspect what lies beneath the outer growth. Then they snip and cut here and there with meticulous precision and planned purpose. And prior to the warmth and new, colorful growth in the spring, they cut back their plants for the cold, grey winter. So it is with our heavenly Gardener and us.

I recall yelling at God one Christmas several decades ago. I had witnessed frightening moments of breaking glass, foul cursing, and physical fighting from my alcoholic stepfather toward my mother. In my anger I screamed at God for His apparent apathy and impotence in straightening out my home. But now, many years later, I see a fuzzy glimpse of what He might have been doing. As a teacher today, I seem to be drawn to students who come from broken and dysfunctional families. Compassion and empathy have blossomed inside me for those who endure alcoholism, abuse, and divorce. Coincidence or God's handiwork? I'll let you decide.

In hindsight, I can even see some good that God has worked from my own adult experiences with divorce.

Through such intense pain, I have come to see how vile and ugly my demanding, selfish flesh can be. I have seen the havoc and hurt it can inflict upon others. Such pruning has brought me closer to realize what Paul realized in Romans 7:24, "What a wretched man I am! Who will rescue me from this body of death?" And that excruciating step led me to the ultimate good news: "Thanks be to God — through Jesus Christ our Lord!" "There is now no condemnation for those who are in Christ Jesus." (Rom. 7:25, 8:1)

In summary then, what is the "good" that God promises to work in all things? It is faith in Jesus, hope in our Father's control, and love for our neighbor. Jesus remained in the Father and bore much fruit. So we also cling ever tighter to our heavenly Vine in times of trials and tribulations and He promises this result: "he will bear much fruit." (John 15:5)

Being pruned with you by the careful Hands of Him who knows what He is doing,

Craig

P.S.

"For we are God's workmanship, created in Christ Jesus to do good works, which He prepared in advance for us to do." (Ephesians 2:10)

"...our great God and Savior, Jesus Christ, who gave Himself for us to redeem us from all wickedness and to purify for Himself a people that are His very own, eager to do what is good." (Titus 2:14)

"Yet, O Lord, you are our Father. We are the clay, you are the potter; we are all the work of your hand." (Isaiah 64:8)

Chapter 2 Questions for Reflection and/or Discussion:

1. Looking back over your life, do you see growth toward Christlikeness?

2. What pruning seasons do you see in your life?

3. An old adage goes something like this: "Be careful what you pray for because you just might get it." If you wanted more patience, for example, what might God give you to forge this fruit?

4. Do you see yourself, in the flesh, as "a wretched person"?

Letter Three

Sometimes I want God to take me home to be with Him. Is that bad?

⁂

D ear Michelle,
A girl in my senior Bible class asked me the same question several years ago. In twenty-two years of teaching I had never been asked that question before. I didn't panic, however, because—like Elijah, Jonah, and Jeremiah before me—I have asked God to take me home. After my divorce was final, I wanted to die.

I asked her what had happened in her life to lead her to such a point. She then described an alcoholic home that had so marred her spirit that she had already determined never to marry and thus torture another soul with putting up with her. Don't misunderstand; she was not suicidal. She was simply at a point very early in life where Paul was in Philippians 1: I would prefer to depart and be with the Lord and leave this mess of a world.

She was struck by the notion that a great apostle had had similar feelings and thoughts. We went to II Corinthians 4 and she nodded in wholehearted agreement that we had found a kindred spirit. Yes, she, too, had felt "hard pressed on every side, perplexed, and struck down." And then she smiled a hope-filled smile. I told her from my perspective she was fighting the good fight of the faith. I didn't know what God was doing in her life, but He was clearly doing something.

Then I marveled at her courage to share such a deep part of her soul with me. I said I was honored and blessed and had never had such a conversation with anyone in my life. And I was amazed at her faith! She still believed, even after having some pretty good reasons to question not only God's existence, but also His power and His benevolence for us. And then we went back to Scripture. So what did Paul conclude?

"For to me, to live is Christ and to die is gain. If I am to go on living in the body, this will mean fruitful labor for me." (Phil. 1:20–21) Now a giddy smile emerged on her face. Her heart was lightening slowly. She was seeing hope. We then went to Gethsemane. I said she reminded me of Jesus. A puzzled look now replaced the smile. I said, "Look at what He prayed in the garden." She already knew. She also knew the conclusion: "not my will, but Thy will be done."

Her life had enormous pain, but it also had eternal purpose. And she could courageously live knowing that God would use her for His purposes and His glory and for the blessing of others through her. I am confident in our great God, Michelle, that He can do the same for you.

But there is another angle to this question I would ask you to reflect upon. Luther wrote that "we should learn to bring our eyes, our hearts, and souls to bear on yonder life in heaven and in a lively hope await it with joy. For if we would be Christians, the ultimate objects of our quest should not be marrying, giving in marriage, buying, selling, planting, building ... But our ultimate quest should be something better and higher, the blessed inheritance in heaven that does not pass away."

I know you feel that your question reveals your weakness. I believe your question shows a growing spiritual maturity! II Corinthians 4:18 urges us to "fix our eyes not on what is seen, but on what is unseen. For what is seen is temporary, but what is unseen is eternal." Listen also to these words from Hebrews 11:13–16: "They admitted that they were aliens and strangers on earth. People who say such things show that they are looking for a country of their own. If they had been thinking of the country they had left, they would have had opportunity to return. Instead, they were longing for a better country—a heavenly one. Therefore God is not ashamed to be called their God, for He has prepared a city for them."

Bear in mind that John ends the entire Bible with the plea for Jesus to return soon. And the Psalmist beautifully pines, "As the deer pants for streams of water, so my soul pants for you, O God. My soul thirsts for God, for the living God. When can I go and meet with God? (Ps. 42:1–2)

Michelle, your question shows me that the Spirit is creating a holy hunger in you. Your soul is thirsty and you realize that the only Thirst Quencher is to be found outside this world. It is not in people, places, possessions, positions, or performances. So, is it bad to desire to be in heaven with our Father? As Paul would emphatically declare in Romans, by no means! Even Augustine quipped, "The whole life of the good Christian is a holy longing." Unfortunately, there are no short cuts to heaven. We must "run with perseverance the race marked out for us." (Heb. 12:1)

So let yourself pine, long, ache, and groan. Let us "fix our eyes on Jesus, the author and perfecter of our faith, who for the joy set before him endured the cross, scorning its shame ... consider him who endured such opposition from sinful men, so that you will not grow weary or lose heart." (Heb. 12:2–3)

More eager to go home than I once was,

Craig

P.S.

"I am going there to prepare a place for you. And if I go to prepare a place for you, I will come back and take you to be with me that you also may be where I am." (John 14:2–3)

"Whom have I in heaven but you? And earth has nothing I desire besides You. My flesh and my heart may fail, but God is the strength of my heart and my portion forever." (Psalm 73:25–26)

Chapter 3 Questions for Reflection and/or Discussion:

1. Are you more eager for heaven than you used to be? If "yes," why?

2. What "quests" in your life have received too much of your focus and energy?

3. In these areas, where exactly have you been tempted to find your life? (People, places, positions, possessions, performances)

4. Explore the traveler analogy. How are we Believers like strangers journeying through a strange land far away from home? What must it have been like for Jesus?

Letter Four

I have such anger at God and others. What can I do?

Dear Michelle,

Anger can be scary. Another's rage can frighten us; our own wrath can alarm us. I liken the emotion to a red warning light on the dashboard of a vehicle. It basically means that something isn't right and that we should stop moving and check things out.

I have always been encouraged by Ephesians 4:26 that says, "In your anger do not sin." The RSV says it more plainly still: "Be angry, but do not sin." Whew! The good news is that anger in and of itself is not necessarily sinful. It can be a very natural, normal, and healthy response. You might have a very good reason for being angry. Perhaps another has greatly harmed you unjustly. Perhaps you have been betrayed or abandoned. Perhaps you have witnessed another being treated unfairly.

I find it interesting that the story of Jesus' anger in the temple is often tiptoed around in Bible studies. Of course, His anger was righteous. He saw that needy people — Gentile worshipers in this case — were being taken advantage of by crass, greedy fortune seekers. Compounding the situation was where it was happening — in His Father's house. A place where needy people could come to find real refuge from a giving and compassionate God had been totally trashed and people were hindered from hearing God's Word.

If your anger is just, then you have One who understands and He invites you to "cast all your anxiety on Him because He cares for you." (I Pet. 5:7) If you have never prayed in such a way as to fully express your feelings before God, let me encourage you to do so. He knows what you are thinking anyway so you might as well say so. The Psalms contain many such expressions and you can probably find a psalm that captures your heart. It might be helpful to pray it over and over.

But the Ephesians verse goes on to say, "Do not sin. Do not let the sun go down while you are still angry and do not give the devil a foothold." The caution here is what we ultimately do with our anger.

Some people feed it. They go around from person to person and share the story of what another did. Most people, even in the church, listen politely and "take sides" with the victim. In this sense, anger can seem to be empowering. But this is deceiving.

Anger is actually a secondary emotion. That is, there is usually something going on in our soul at a deeper level that needs examining. In my life, I have found that the deeper issues are often hurt or fear. When I catch myself being upset, I have found it helpful to get quiet and ask God to "test my anxious heart and to show me if there is any offensive way in me." (Ps. 139:23–24) And God usually shows me. I sometimes ask myself, "What am I scared of happening here?" "Why do I feel hurt?"

John Eldredge, an insightful author whose writings are in the bibliography, said that we should take time daily to grieve. *(The Journey of Desire)* Whereas most people try to avoid pain and feeling sad or hurt, he said we should embrace suffering. I think I know why. When we stop to consider how another has failed us, it leads us to an unsettling conclusion: no one down here can give me what my heart deeply desires—unfailing love. (Prov. 19:22a) No matter how loving or kind my parents or spouse or friends have been, there is no one on earth who is consistently, totally, unconditionally sold out for me. The refreshing and liberating Truth is that there is One who has unfailing love for me. My mind knows this but my flesh usually runs after lesser lovers and then I am disappointed when they fail me. The disappointment serves as a painful but necessary reminder of where my life is really hidden.

For example, when I realize that beneath my anger is great fear that my son will never be close to me or that I will lose my position if I get divorced, I slowly begin to see my idolatry. I see how I exchanged Godly desires for ungodly goals, how I traded the truth ("I would like...") for a lie ("I NEED..."). The bottom line is this: only One thing is needful. (Lk. 10:42) But I will never see these truths if I feed my anger. I will never see these truths if I seek out others who will help me feed my anger. I will never see these truths if I seek revenge or harbor bitter resentment. (*Finding God*)

I have experienced God melt my anger when He has reminded me of these facts: 1) God is all I truly need, and 2) God has forgiven me much. If I am honest, my debt that He canceled is infinitely greater than any debt owed me by another in this life. And, if I truly understand my position in the grand scheme of things, I will admit that I have no right to demand anything from another, myself, or God. On a quick side note, my bouts with anger have slowly led me to look for what lies beneath others' anger. Rather than be intimidated by their strong emotion, I try to look for the hurt or fear behind it.

So, what should you do with anger? I suggest that you examine your feelings and beliefs behind it. Check for demandingness. Ask the Lord to show you any idolatry. (Ps. 139:23–24) Repent and rest in His forgiveness. And quietly trust that He will have the vengeance if justly required. Oh, and one more thought on the matter: don't be surprised if you need to do this repeatedly within a day or a week or a month. Our demanding flesh rears its ugly head at every opportunity. It will die very slowly. But be assured that it has indeed been put to death.

More content than I used to be but not as much as I want to be,

Craig

P.S.

"Everyone should be quick to listen, slow to

speak and slow to become angry, for man's anger does not bring about the righteous life that God desires." (James 1:19–20)

"But he who has been forgiven little loves little." (Luke 7:47b)

"The Lord is compassionate and gracious, slow to anger, abounding in love. He will not always accuse, nor will He harbor His anger forever." (Psalm 103:8–9)

Chapter 4 Questions for Reflection and/or Discussion:

1. With whom are you currently angry? Why?

2. Our times of being upset can be windows to our soul. Think of recent times you were upset. What were you demanding of another? yourself? God?

3. What do you greatly fear? (i.e. Growing old alone, having a horrible accident, etc.)

4. Think of past occurrences of anger in your life. Were you believing that you NEEDED something rather than merely desiring it?

Is God punishing me for some past sin?

D ear Michelle,
I really feel for you today. Your question is close to another one asked two thousand years ago on a cross, "My God, my God, why have you forsaken me?" I am sure that it seems like God is angry with you and that He must be zapping you for some past or present sin in thought, word, or deed. The world often misrepresents God as some cosmic killjoy, a policeman who jumps on our every misstep. The cross tells us a different story.

All our sins—past, present, and future—were nailed on the cross with Jesus. He was spanked, if you will, for us, once and for all, then and there. For us to be punished now would be to say that what Jesus did was not sufficient. And that would be blasphemy. Luther drives home the point by saying, "How could He be angry with us who died for us?

Therefore although He appears to be angry, it is nonetheless not true that He is angry."

Psalm 103:10 beautifully assures us that "He does not treat us as our sins deserve or repay us according to our iniquities." Do you know what it would mean for us if He did? Instantaneous death! Descent into hell! Eternal separation from Him! No, Michelle, God is not punishing you for some past sin. But I believe He is sanctifying you, as He is sanctifying all the saints on earth. What does this mean?

As usual, it is best if I let God speak for Himself here. Notice the same theme from four different places in His Word: "See, I have refined you, though not as silver; I have tested you in the furnace of affliction." (Isaiah 48:10) "God disciplines us for our good, that we may share in His holiness. No discipline seems pleasant at the time, but painful. Later on, however, it produces a harvest of righteousness and peace for those who have been trained by it." (Heb. 12:10b–11) "Though now for a little while you may have had to suffer grief in all kinds of trials. These have come so that your faith—of greater worth than gold, which perishes even though refined by fire—may be proved genuine and may result in praise, glory, and honor when Jesus Christ is revealed." (I Pet. 1:6b–7) "He cuts off every branch in me that bears no fruit, while every branch that does bear fruit He prunes so that it will be even more fruitful." (John 15:2)

This discipline is not fun. But it is important to remind ourselves often that "the Lord disciplines those He loves." (Heb. 12:6) And we have a very rebellious flesh; we have many rough edges; we have much dross that needs to be burnt off. Again Luther reminds us, "The ultimate purpose of afflictions is the mortification of the flesh, the expulsion of sins, and the checking of that original evil which is embedded in our nature. And the more you are cleansed, the more will you be blessed in the future life...For when we enjoy peace and rest, we do not pray, we do not meditate on the Word but deal coldly with Scriptures and everything that pertains to God."

I have found a law in life that seems to work hand-in-hand with God's design of sanctification. Galatians 6:7b–8 tells us, "A man reaps what he sows. The one who sows to please his sinful nature, from that nature will reap destruction." A good and faithful Christian friend asked me once what had drawn me to marry another so quickly after my divorce. Embarrassed and ashamed, I had to admit some fleshly reasons. Those reasons were not very loving to my second spouse nor were they a good foundation on which to build a relationship. The rest of the story is I reaped what I sowed and that marriage, too, ended in disaster.

Author Peter Kreeft has remarked that this world is not a very good home but it makes for a fine gymnasium. (*Making Sense Out of Suffering*) It is a helpful image for me to remember that life down here is for training purposes. God wants to make little Christs to glorify Him and love others. I think Luther summarizes this chapter pretty well with the following: "God chastises and disciplines those whom He intends to keep and preserve for eternal life. One man has this trouble, another man has a different trouble from which he would gladly be relieved. God is acting in your best interests, to keep you in His fear and drive you to the Word and prayer." And that is always a good place for us to be.

Fully forgiven and completely righteous in Christ with you,

Craig

P.S.

"He does not treat us as our sins deserve or repay us according to our iniquities." (Psalm 103:10)

"For we know that our old self was crucified with Him so that the body of sin might be done away with, that we should no longer be slaves to sin." (Romans 6:6)

"Therefore, there is now no condemnation for those who are in Christ Jesus." (Romans 8:1)

"If you, O Lord, kept a record of sins, O Lord, who could stand?" (Psalm 130:3)

"In repentance and rest is your salvation; in quietness and trust is your strength." (Isaiah 30:15a)

Chapter 5 Questions for Reflection and/or Discussion:

1. Do you have a past sin that is difficult for you to feel free of guilt or condemnation?

2. Which is more trustworthy, your feelings or God's Word? Why?

3. James 5:16 tells us to confess our sins to one another and to pray for one another. Have you ever confessed your deepest, darkest sins to a trusted believer? If "yes," what happened? If "no," with whom could you?

4. We reap what we sow. What consequences have resulted due to some of your sins?

Letter Six

With such troubling doubts and fears, am I still a Christian?

Dear Michelle,
Unfortunately, it is quite common in the church today for people to parade about as if they had no worries or wonderings. As a sign of "strong faith," people seem to put on airs that they have a firm hold on life. Compound this false front with the fact that very few people — even Christians — risk getting close enough to others to become naked before them. What if they find out what I am really like? What if they see that I am really a small, frightened little boy inside a man's body? What if they discover the intense struggles I have with vile thoughts? What if they discover how much I don't know and how much uncertainty lies within my heart over the things I think I know?

A Christian counselor once opened my eyes with the words, "I would rather be a sincere, mediocre Christian than a fake good one." As I have traveled a little farther down life's path, I have discovered that "real" people don't have all the answers. They don't even flinch when they say, "I don't know." It's as if they have grown more comfortable than the "average" human with life's mysteries. And almost without exception, the most real people I have met have experienced seasons of intense suffering and doubting.

One of the most profound and influential persons in my life (yes, he was a friend with whom my soul was stripped bare) told me that life is a good proving ground for faith. He encouraged me to let myself feel pain and to admit fears. He said the more I long, ache, and groan, the more I will thirst for God and the next world. He was right.

By now perhaps you are beginning to see that doubts and fears can draw us closer to, rather than drive us farther from, God. We often have a misguided view of growth. We think it means feeling better or improving somehow. Growth might be seeing ourselves more and more as God sees us and accepting ourselves as God accepts us in Christ. We are no longer under condemnation (Rom. 8:1) and we are "without blemish and free from accusation." (Col. 1:22)

Rather than resting in answers, we should be even more content to rest in Him who has all the answers! There is a profound difference between the two. The former will not quench our thirst or lead us to peace. "Let not the wise man boast of his wisdom or the strong man boast of his strength or the rich man boast of his riches, but let him who boasts boast about this: that he understands and knows me."

(Jer. 9:23–24a) Later Jeremiah declares God's promise, "You will seek me and find me when you seek me with all your heart." (Jer. 29:13) In my life, I have more fervently sought after God when I was beset with all sorts of troubling doubts and fears. A cursory glance at Scripture will reveal that you and I are in good company.

Jeremiah, Job, David, Moses, Abraham, and Paul all faced huge question marks in their lives. Three times Paul asked God to take away his thorn in the flesh. God merely responded with, "My grace is sufficient for you, for my power is made perfect in weakness." (II Cor. 12:9) Paul decided to boast in his weaknesses so that Christ's power might rest on him. He concluded that when he had come to the end of his own resources, it was then that he had found his real strength in Christ. You seem to be in a similar place, Michelle. Perhaps you pray often what the father with the possessed son asked of Jesus, "I do believe; help me overcome my unbelief!" (Mark 9:24) I know it has been a favorite petition of mine over the years.

Your question leads us to one of the least discussed truths about our Christian journey in this world: we are at war. Far from the misguided worldly view that Christianity is just another path to peace and prosperity in this life, the real story of a Christian is often the opposite. Our sinful flesh and new spirit rage against each other within us. Inner tension and turmoil persist in the minds and hearts of Christians fighting the good fight. Contradictions and conflicting voices are all around. Romans 7:14–25 is an excellent description of this battle. This struggle, this back-and-forth teeter tottering, is not experienced by unbelieving captives, P.O.W.'s (prisoners of the world). Think about the implications of this last statement and your question, Michelle.

Be on guard against this temptation from the flesh: putting faith in your faith. The object of our faith — Jesus — is far more important than the amount of faith we have. As Paul says in II Corinthians 3:5: "Not that we are competent in ourselves to claim anything for ourselves, but our competence comes from God." This is also why Matthew writes, "I tell you the truth, if you have faith as small as a mustard seed, you can say to this mountain, 'Move from here to there' and it will move." (Matthew 17:20)

I like to use this analogy with students. If half the class put great, infinite trust in me to take a calculus test for them (I didn't advance beyond algebra!), and the other half put feeble, hardly visible trust in the class valedictorian, who would be better off after the tests are graded? Look at the One in whom you and I place our weak and puny faith. He created this universe by speaking. He sent a worldwide flood. He walked on water. He raised the dead. He rose from the dead. And He invites you and me to cast all our cares on Him for He cares about us! (I Peter 5:7) And He promises, after we have presented our requests to Him, that His peace will guard our hearts and minds in Christ Jesus. (Philippians 4:6–7) He is faithful and He will do it.

I hope in my next letter to delve further into your concern. For now, let us cling to God's precious promises in His Word.

Your fellow warrior, sometimes battered and bloodied, but always and ultimately on the winning side,

Craig

P.S.

"The Lord is close to the brokenhearted and saves those who are crushed in spirit. A righteous man may have many troubles, but the Lord delivers him from them all." (Psalm 34:18–19)

"A bruised reed he will not break, and a smoldering wick he will not snuff out." (Matthew 12:20)

Chapter 6 Questions for Reflection and/or Discussion:

1. What "real" people do you know?

2. How genuine or honest are you with others about your doubts, fears, and struggles?

3. What do you think it means to "put faith in your faith"?

4. Paul said he fought the good fight. What battles are you now fighting because you are a Christian?

Letter Seven

I am afraid of losing my faith. How can I prevent that?

◆

Dear Michelle,
To lose one's faith is the scariest thought for us to have. After all, it has eternal consequences. To lose our Savior and Lord is to lose everything. Without Him we have nothing: no love, no hope, no joy, no peace, no future, no purpose. And, yet, the fact that you are now struggling with such a fear, I think, is a good sign. It shows that you know what is most important in life. You know that something far worse could happen to you than your present tribulation.

You have pinpointed the heart of the real fight in this world: am I going to trust myself or trust God? Our flesh is always seeking the program that works or the plan that is foolproof. It is a subtle effort to avoid having to lean on God, even if we piously ask Him to show us the way. He IS the way. (John 14:6) It is so easy to forget that fact.

What suffering eventually shows us is that we can't control our life. We can't control others. We can't control circumstances. Such a proposition is at first extremely frightening. (Remember, we creatures like to feel in control!) However, over time such realization liberates us adopted children to trust God and love others. Our time and energy is much better utilized doing those two things than trying to do the impossible: control the uncontrollable.

Looking to our weak selves and our own feeble efforts would guarantee nothing but uncertainty ("Have I done enough?") or despair ("I can't do what needs to be done!"). Granted, there might be moments of pride when we experience brief successes of meeting some legalistic standard. Eventually, however, we will second-guess even our best efforts. So, is it clear that **we** can't prevent ourselves, or anyone else for that matter, from losing faith? The Good News is that "what is impossible with men is possible with God." (Lk. 18:27) Fortunately, He has given us some pretty weighty assurances in His Word.

> "I give them eternal life, and they shall never perish; no one can snatch them out of my hand. My Father, who has given them to me, is greater than all; no one can snatch them out of my Father's hand." (John 10:28–29)

"He will keep you strong to the end, so that you will be blameless on the day of our Lord Jesus Christ." (I Cor. 1:8)

"Now it is God who makes both us and you stand firm in Christ. He anointed us, set his seal of ownership on us, and put his Spirit in our hearts as a deposit, guaranteeing what is to come." (II Cor. 1:21–22)

"Let us fix our eyes on Jesus, the author and perfecter of our faith." (Heb. 12:2a)

"Being confident of this, that he who began a good work in you will carry it on to completion until the day of Christ Jesus." (Phil. 1:6)

Our salvation, from start to finish, seems to be God's doing and responsibility. That is a good thing! With men it would be impossible, but with God all things are possible. (Mt. 19:26) The evil one is always trying to worm his way in and steal some of the glory from God. Satan appeals to our fleshly pride and tempts us to think that we contribute, that we earn, that we have something to do with being saved. Listen to Paul, "It is because of him that you are in Christ Jesus, who has become for us wisdom from God — that is, our righteousness, holiness, and redemption. Therefore, as it is written, 'Let him who boasts boast in the Lord.'" (I Cor. 1:30–31)

I have a final thought on this question, Michelle. If you read the first chapter of Genesis slowly, especially verses 3, 6, 7, 9, 11, 14, 15, you will notice a repeating pattern of "And God said" followed closely by "And it was so." After almost ten years of teaching that chapter to high school seniors, it finally dawned on me that such a claim can be made only by God. Think about it: if God says something, it will happen. I can't make that claim, for I have broken some promises. I don't know another human being who can make that claim either. Sometimes people have good reasons for not following through on statements made. Illness or bad weather or fatigue or simple forgetfulness wipes out a good intention. And sometimes people have poor reasons for not following through: vengeance, selfishness, and payback come to mind. Not so with God. He is forever faithful and totally trustworthy.

You and I may rest in His loving arms as we go to sleep tonight. The pressure is off. Jesus is carrying our burdens. He has said it, and He will do it!

Being held with you in His grip of grace,

Craig

P.S.

"And my God will meet all your needs according to his glorious riches in Christ Jesus." (Philippians 4:19)

"He who did not spare his own Son, but gave him up for us all—how will he not also, along with him, graciously give us all things?" (Romans 8:32)

Chapter 7 Questions for Reflection and/or Discussion:

1. It can be frightening or liberating to realize we don't exert as much control in our lives as we like to think we do. What is your reaction?

2. Which Scriptural promise in this chapter is most comforting to you? Why?

3. What promises have you broken in your life?

4. What promises made by others to you have been broken?

Letter Eight

I have such pain.
How can I endure the
hurt without sinning?

Dear Michelle,
Pain can certainly turn us inward, can't it? It can lead us to hide from God and from others. Of course, by retreating we are also hiding from ourselves and from our purpose for being here in the first place. The liar satan is murdering us by deceiving us. (Jn. 8:44b)

There are two ways that our flesh is wired to handle pain: to deny it or to obsess over it. Both approaches, at first, appear to promise relief. But as we traverse the path that once seemed so smooth, we eventually find ourselves dangling on a dangerous cliff. Our recovery period will be greatly lengthened by these two "escapes" and neither path will invite us to be very loving toward others. Ultimately, of course, each route leads us farther and farther away from

God.

The world uses various methods to deny pain. Many avenues are notorious and are seen by society at large as unhealthy. Among these are such things as illicit drugs, promiscuous sex, and abused alcohol. There are some apparently less harmful behaviors that people use to numb the intense pain from some trial: eating, reading, viewing, shopping, working, exercising, and hobbying. A careful inventory is helpful, albeit often convicting, to see if we are succumbing to one of these forms of denial. While these gifts from God are to be received with thanksgiving and to be enjoyed within certain boundaries, all of them can easily become an idol.

You might recall that an idol is whatever we fear, love, and trust above all things. Luther said, "A god is that from which we are to expect everything good and to which we are to take refuge in all times of need." What we do often shows what we believe. Therefore it is helpful to periodically stop and examine ourselves. What activities are getting the most time and energy (and maybe money) from me? What times of day do I engage in these behaviors? What is my emotional state during those times? What does my heart deeply desire to gain?

Author John Eldredge (*The Journey of Desire*) advises staying with the desire ten minutes longer before acting upon it. I have found that when I pray Psalm 139:23–24 God shows me deeper truths. "Search me, O God, and know my heart; test me and know my anxious thoughts. See if there is any offensive way in me, and lead me in the way everlasting." I usually see that I am really desiring something deeper than sex or food. If I lie down and pray and think about what I really desire, I discover that I really want an intimacy or acceptance or security that no one and no thing on this earth can give me. And that leads me back to our Lord, who is the everlasting way to all these things and more.

The other fleshly path is to obsess over our pain. This results when we can think of little else. We make the pain *the* defining aspect of our lives. We are driven to find a cure, explore the causes, and fix the problem. So we spend countless hours with a popular counselor or a self-help book or a promising conference. We try feeding ourselves with positive thoughts. We find what we are good at and build our self-esteem. We experiment with communication techniques or physical exercises or new medication. We unearth what happened and went wrong in our childhood homes. And we might even invoke God's assistance, like a janitor hired to clean up messes, in each endeavor.

Rather than seeking God with all our heart, we pursue these otherwise good — albeit limited — pursuits with all our heart. We chase all avenues with desperation like a man thirsty for water in a barren desert. Unfortunately, all these will eventually show themselves for what they are — leaky wells. (*Finding God*) And what will be the result of drinking from them? We will be even more thirsty, lonely, and bitter.

Such an approach assumes that if we find ourselves we can correct and amend whatever needs adjusting. It reminds me of some of the hardest words in Scripture I have ever swallowed: "For whoever wants to save his life will lose it, but whoever loses his life for me will find it."

(Mt. 16: 25) Jesus is our life. (John 14:6) If we think our life is hidden anywhere else, (Col. 3:3) then we are sorely mistaken. And the deception is very similar to the first one presented to Eve in the garden. The tree looked good to eat. What can possibly be wrong with trying to save a marriage? What is wrong with prolonging good health? What is wrong with storing up wealth for unseen expenses? What is wrong with seeking emotional well-being? It all depends upon our prioritizing. The daily struggle down here in this fallen world, saddled with the filthy, rotting maggot sack flesh (Luther's description) is keeping first things first. And God is always first.

We casually and unconsciously throw around the possessive pronoun "my." We brazenly attach it to so many things near us: spouse, children, health, job, house, wealth. But "the earth is the Lord's, and everything in it, the world, and all who live in it." (Ps. 24:1) Nothing is truly ours. We are not even our own. We have been bought with a price. (I Cor. 6:19) I wonder what would happen if you started thinking that your present trial is God's. It is *His* health, not mine. That other person is *His*, not mine. The future is in *His* hands, not mine.

As you can probably now see, we will inevitably sin in the midst of our pain. We will, at times, turn inward and move away from others and from God. But we know what to do with sin: confess it; admit it; despise it. Lay it at the foot of the cross. And then receive the forgiveness won by Jesus at that cross. And then I think God will slowly, gradually, begin to increase our perseverance and endurance. He will mold and shape our character, conforming it more and more like that of Jesus' so that we, too, can become people of many sorrows, well acquainted with grief. We, too, will pray many prayers with sobbing. And our hearts will more and more desire that His will be done in the midst of our tribulations and that our will take a back seat.

To accept pain, and not deny it or obsess over it, is to trust God. Rather than seeking solutions with all our might, we will be caught up in the nobler, better pursuit of seeking a closer relationship with God. In the midst of agony, we will thank God for He is good. And we will trust His goodness. And we will be more committed to exalting Jesus in our lives than in making our lives happier. And good will overcome evil as we concentrate more on giving to others than on relieving our pain.

God's primary work now — in all things — is to work for His children's good, conforming us more and more into the image of Jesus. He sanctifies us by His Word of truth and by the cauldron of trials. The potter needs to remove some clay. The precious gold must first be melted to burn away impurities. We must suffer.

May the Spirit direct us to the Father's love and to the perseverance of Christ,

Craig

P.S.

"I will cleanse you from all your impurities and from all your idols. I will give you a new heart and put a new spirit in you; I will remove from you your heart of stone and give you a heart of flesh. And I will put my Spirit in you and move you to follow my decrees and be careful to keep my laws." (Ezekiel 36:25b–27)

"In repentance and rest is your salvation, in quietness and trust is your strength." (Isaiah 30:15a)

"My dear children, I write this to you so that you will not sin. But if anybody does sin, we have one who speaks to the Father in our defense — Jesus Christ, the Righteous One. He is the atoning sacrifice for our sins, and not only for ours but also for the sins of the whole world." (I John 2:1–2)

Chapter 8 Questions for Reflection and/or Discussion:

1. How are you tempted to numb pain in your life? (That is, what "sedatives" do you use?)

2. How are you tempted to obsess over your pain? (Don't forget to check your conversations.)

3. Where have you been tempted to believe your life is hidden?

4. Do you find yourself crying more easily now than you did earlier in your life?

Letter Nine

How much longer
will this trial last?

Dear Michelle,
You certainly are a kindred spirit with the psalmist!
Many psalms echo your plea. Here are a couple of my
favorite ones:

> "My soul is in anguish. How long, O Lord,
> how long? … I am worn out from groaning; all
> night long I flood my bed with weeping and
> drench my couch with tears." (Ps. 6:3, 6)

> "How long, O Lord? Will you forget me
> forever? How long will you hide your face from
> me? How long must I wrestle with my thoughts
> and every day have sorrow in my heart?"
> (Ps. 13:1–2)

In our society of quick fixes, we are an impatient people. Microwaves heat our food in seconds, pills remove our headaches within minutes, and tablets soothe our stomachaches in an hour. Our McDonalds-Drive-Thru world does not teach us patience. Henry David Thoreau said that we all scurry about like ants down here. I think that is pretty much true. And we expect, even have the audacity to demand, that God do likewise.

But this leads me to another fascinating observation about Jesus: He never seemed to be in a hurry. I don't recall any event where He was running. John 11:3–6 tells us a most revealing story on this point. "So the sisters sent word to Jesus, 'Lord, the one you love is sick.' When he heard this, Jesus said, 'This sickness will not end in death. No, it is for God's glory so that God's Son may be glorified through it.' Jesus loved Martha and her sister and Lazarus. Yet when he heard that Lazarus was sick, he stayed where he was two more days."

I imagine that those two days were excruciatingly long and agonizing for the sisters. You might recall the rest of the story. Lazarus dies and Jesus eventually raises him from the dead. I believe this story teaches us several lessons.

First, God moves on a completely different timetable than you and I do. He knows what you and I do not know—the rest of the story! Mary and Martha certainly couldn't see into the future and neither can we. We are shortsighted and narrow-minded. It would be helpful for us to remind ourselves of this fact from time to time. I suspect that my flesh is similar to yours, Michelle. God's timetable is always too slow for my comfort, but it is always just right for my good.

A second lesson is a most amazing sentence inserted in the middle of this story. In between where Jesus is sought after and when He finally travels to their home, we read these words: "Jesus loved Martha and her sister and Lazarus." Miles away the ladies are grieving at the deathbed of their brother. The young man is vainly fighting for his life. From their perspective, God is doing nothing. To them He appears to be silent, unresponsive, uncaring. But that is not what the text tells us. God's Word tells us plainly, Jesus loves them in His delaying. And right now, like Martha and Mary, you want Jesus to come to you and to act today. But you don't see Him yet and you wonder what is taking Him so long. Be assured He loves you even today, even in His silence.

A final lesson is the point behind the smaller story. The smaller story, of course, is that Lazarus is dying. I know that doesn't seem small and I am sure it didn't seem minor to Martha or to Mary or especially to Lazarus! But this text tells us the reason for the sickness. "It is for God's glory so that God's Son may be glorified through it." That is a pretty big story in which to be cast as a major character. That has eternal significance. Luther knew this too: "A person may be poor, sick, miserable, and despised and yet be saved, as happens to all Christians. Yet he should make his will depend on the will of God; if the desired help does not serve God's glory, or is disadvantageous to our salvation, we should be glad to bear the cross longer."

I heard the following story somewhere and I think it applies to your question. When gold is purified, it is placed in fire and the heat is intensified. However, the goldsmith must be careful to maintain the exact temperature for the exact length of time so the gold isn't ruined. When asked how he knows when it is time to remove the gold from the fire, one man answered, "When I can see my image reflected in it."

Michelle, I don't know how much longer you must endure the fire of your trial. It might be days or weeks or months or even years. But you and I both know that He knows. And He knows exactly what He is doing for your good and His glory.

The answer the Psalms give us is a recurring refrain in the Old Testament: "Wait for the Lord; be strong and take heart and wait for the Lord." (Ps. 27:14) I have found great comfort in Psalm 13. As you recall, we began this chapter with a quote from the beginning of that Psalm, "How long, O Lord? Will you forget me forever?" Notice how the psalm ends in just five short verses later, "But I trust in your unfailing love; my heart rejoices in your salvation. I will sing to the Lord, for he has been good to me." (Ps. 13:5–6) We can ask your question, Michelle, and long for God's deliverance. We can be at what we think is our breaking point where we can't take another minute of pain. And, yet, we can still, in the midst of all those powerful feelings, trust in God's unfailing love!

Waiting on the Lord with you,

Craig

P.S.

"I waited patiently for the Lord; he turned to

me and heard my cry. He lifted me out of the slimy pit, out of the mud and mire; he set my feet on a rock and gave me a firm place to stand." (Psalm 40:1–2)

"Be merciful to me, O Lord, for I am in distress; my eyes grow weak with sorrow, my soul and my body with grief. My life is consumed by anguish and my years by groaning; my strength fails because of my affliction, and my bones grow weak … But I trust in you, O Lord; I say, 'You are my God.' My times are in your hands." (Psalm 31:9–10, 14–15a)

"Yet the Lord longs to be gracious to you; he rises to show you compassion. For the Lord is a God of justice. Blessed are all who wait for him!" (Isaiah 30:18)

Chapter 9 Questions for Reflection and/or Discussion:

1. Think of things that you have had to wait for in your life. What might have happened if you had received some of those things earlier than you did? later?

2. Think of times when you have had to endure grueling conditions to achieve some end. Were you part of some team or group in school? Have you succeeded in some difficult course of study? Have you achieved some arduous project at work? What were those times like? Looking back, were they worth the struggle?

3. Some people think there is a Bible verse that says, "God will never give you more than you can handle." (There actually is no such verse.) Read II Corinthians 1:8–9. How should this statement be truthfully rephrased?

4. We Christians believe we will live for eternity. Why do you think we live our lives in such a hurry?

Letter Ten

Does God really answer prayer?

D ear Michelle,
I well remember the days—and nights—that I wondered the same thing. I recalled all the special promises in Scripture, promises such as "Ask and it will be given to you" (Mt. 7:7) and "I will do whatever you ask in my name." (Jn. 14:13) I recall feeling betrayed and set up for, as I thought at the time, surely these words are not true. Fortunately, the Spirit convinced my reason that if I believed God was wrong, or worse, lying, then perhaps I didn't fully understand what He was saying. This led me to search intently with an earnestness that I had never—prior to that moment in time—approached God's Word. I think this was the deepest and darkest battle in my spiritual crisis. After all, if we can't trust God, then whom can we trust? In the words of Peter, "Lord, to whom shall we go? You have the

words of eternal life." (Jn. 6:68) And here I was facing my worst possible fear: God doesn't really care for me and this whole Christianity business is one big hoax.

The answer to our query hinges on what we mean by "answer". Of course, at that point I more zealously than today believed that I was the center of the universe. I thought that I was the point and that God's role was to assist me in making my life as pleasant and as happy as possible. He existed for me and not vice versa. I not only assumed that I knew what I should pray for, but I also believed I knew what the forthcoming answer should be!

As I write these words now, such a position really sounds ridiculous and not a little conceited to me. I intellectually knew from confirmation days that God, and not I, was omniscient. After all, He has the vantage point of eternity while I see "but a poor reflection as in a mirror." (I Cor. 13:12) Then I came across Paul's letter to the Romans: "...the Spirit helps us in our weakness. We do not know what we ought to pray for, but the Spirit himself intercedes for us with groans that words cannot express. And he who searches our hearts knows the mind of the Spirit, because the Spirit intercedes for the saints in accordance with God's will." (Rom. 8:26–27) This opened my eyes to several revelations.

First, I really didn't know how to pray or for what I should pray. I am embarrassed to say how old I was and how many years I had taught in a Christian school before this thought really pierced my soul. I remembered that the disciples had asked Jesus to teach them to pray. For the first time in my life, I wanted to learn that lesson too.

The second revelation shown me by the Spirit was that I was a spoiled, two-year old brat, demanding this toy and that one from my Father. I desired the gifts over the Giver. I saw God as a mere blessing dispenser and not as a person who was zealously concerned for me as a person. I thought His job was to make my life here happy. I didn't realize that He intensely desired to give me the greatest gift of all— Himself in an intimate and loving relationship. Needless to say, my conception of "the abundant life" Jesus offered radically changed.

The third revelation that I learned following this abrupt spanking by the law was pure, sweet Gospel: I had an Intercessor who could communicate from the depth of my heart to God's! That comforted me greatly for there were many times that I couldn't even put words to a prayer. I was mute. And when I would finally utter some nonsense or other, I could count on that Intercessor interpreting my real desire, even if it flew in the face of what I thought I needed.

But the fourth revelation leveled me to the core. It became painfully obvious to me that I had not prayed in accordance with God's will. Even though I said the right words, I wasn't even remotely interested in God's will. I didn't want Jesus to be exalted in my life; I wanted to be exalted. I didn't want to surrender all and admit that nothing was mine; I was busy clutching and grabbing. Today I am thankful that God did not answer many of my prayers as I desired them to be answered.

Luther provided further insight that confirmed these revelations. "God does not always do what we desire but does what is beneficial for us. For since God is good, He can give nothing but what is good. However, we often ask for our children, often for our friends, often for ourselves, not what is good but what seems to us to be good. In such cases God grants our prayer even when He does not do what we ask ... if the desired help does not serve God's glory, or is disadvantageous to our salvation, we should be glad to bear the cross longer ... For we are fools and do not know what we should ask for."

A most amazing and miraculous thing then began to happen that I can only attribute to God's doing: I began to give thanks to the Lord for He is good. It was a prayer my family said together after most meals but now it was as if fireworks were exploding around the words. The realization was slowly sinking in: God IS good and I should thank Him. God's Word became living and active in my heart. I Thess. 5:17–18 came to mind over and over, "pray continually; give thanks in all circumstances, for this is God's will for you in Christ Jesus." I could now do two things that were clearly God's will: pray often and thank Him IN (not necessarily FOR) all circumstances. Only one prayer made sense to me: "Thy will be done and thanks, God!"

This was no small transformation moving from practically accusing God of lying and insisting on my own way to desiring to place circumstances and every part of my life in His hands. Today, like Luther, I feel that I never pray better than when I am in trouble. God is indeed "at work in us both to will and to act according to his good purpose." (Phil. 2:13)

I think the clincher for me was knowing that God Himself knew how I felt. It is okay to make a request of

God as we desire. But our prayer dare not stop there. "He fell with his face to the ground and prayed, 'My Father, if it is possible, may this cup be taken from me. Yet, not as I will, but as you will.'" (Mt. 26:39) Such a prayer was uttered in sheer agony with drops of blood. By the power of the Spirit in you, Michelle, you, too, can pray the same prayer in your Gethsemane experience you now have. If you do, you will see that God indeed really answers prayer.

May we always pray the classical hymn, "Heart of my own heart, whatever befall, still be my vision, O Ruler of all."

Craig

P.S.

"Now to him who is able to do immeasurably more than all we ask or imagine, according to his power that is at work within us, to him be glory in the church and in Christ Jesus throughout all generations, Forever and ever! Amen." (Ephesians 3:20–21)

"Do not be anxious about anything, but in everything, by prayer and petition, with thanksgiving, present your requests to God. And the peace of God, which transcends all understanding, will guard your hearts and your minds in Christ Jesus." (Philippians 4:6–7)

"I waited patiently for the Lord; he turned to

me and heard my cry. He lifted me out of the slimy pit, out of the mud and mire; he set my feet on a rock and gave me a firm place to stand. He put a new song in my mouth, a hymn of praise to our God. Many will see and fear and put their trust in the Lord." (Psalm 4:1–3)

Chapter 10 Questions For Reflection And/Or Discussion:

1. What major prayers of yours have not been answered as you desired?

2. How often do you earnestly pray, "Thy will be done"?

3. How often do you give thanks to God?

4. For what can you give God thanks in your present circumstances?

I don't feel like praying, worshiping, or reading the Bible. What should I do?

Dear Michelle,
This is one battle that I imagine each and every Christian is familiar with. When it comes to the subject of feelings, you are certainly not alone here. In fact, this is a dominant theme in our American culture today: "If it feels good, do it." The inverse is, of course, if it feels bad, don't do it. If you think about it, this idolatry—fearing, loving, and trusting our feelings above all things—is a dangerous lie that can lead only to trouble.

Imagine how little good would actually occur if everyone merely followed their feelings. I venture to say that the vast majority of adults would never go to work, the vast majority of students would never go to school, and the vast majority of people would never love another person. As an example, consider how much parents—contrary to their feelings—do for their children. I doubt if the average parent really *feels* like waking from peaceful slumber at 2:00 a.m. to feed the screaming little tyke in the next room. So why do they? It is simply a matter of the will.

Ah, but I sense in your question perhaps a deeper, more honest, question: "But what if I don't really *want* to?" That I appreciate. Again, Michelle, this dark night of your soul is taking you to depths that you never dreamed of seeing. It is as if we are onions and we are suffering the peeling of layer after layer of pretense and deception. As we become more naked, we fear if anything called "us" will be left. It feels like a slow, cruel death. And in a real sense, it is. Our flesh is being put to death. We begin to see that fleshly ways are worn out; they really don't work. We begin to see how depraved, how corrupt to the core, we really are. We don't have problems as much as we ARE the problem! In the final analysis, I must admit that my flesh doesn't want to worship, pray, or read. My flesh doesn't want any part of God.

You wonder what can you do? By now, it is probably painfully obvious that you can't do anything. But that is a very good place to be. To be depleted, empty, and void makes it clear to us, and to those near us, that if something is going to happen, it is going to be by God's might. And with Him all things are possible. As Paul tells us in Philippians 2:13, "For it is God who works in you to will and to act according to his good purpose." The Psalmist put it this way, "Delight yourself in the Lord and he will give you the desires of your heart." (Ps. 37:4) More than once have many other believers and I prayed, "Lord, give me the want to. Give me the desire to do such and such." And God is faithful.

I suppose these feelings lead you to some other uncomfortable feelings too. Perhaps you don't feel very much like a Christian. It is helpful to remember here, fortunately, that our faith is dependent upon some real life facts, not feelings. Christ died for us. (Rom. 5:8) The Spirit dwells within us. (I Cor. 6:19) We have been baptized. (Rom. 6:3) We are in Christ. (Rom. 8:1) We are dearly loved children of God. (I Jn. 3:1) We are complete in Him. (Col. 2:10) But these truths are so easy to forget. It is so easy to focus our eyes on our feelings or our faith rather than on Jesus. Beware of putting faith in your faith. That will lead either to pride or to despair.

Perhaps you don't feel very worthy in God's sight. Who among us is worthy? Again, look to Jesus and not to yourself. "But now he has reconciled you by Christ's physical body through death to present you holy in his sight, without blemish and free from accusation." (Col. 1:22) "It is because of him you are in Christ Jesus, who has become for us wisdom from God—that is, our righteousness, holiness and redemption." (I Cor. 1:30) In what is known as the great exchange, Jesus took our sinfulness and gave us His righteousness. Through Him, you and I are worthy and can approach the throne of God the Father with confidence.

Perhaps you feel as though there is a scarlet "L" tattooed to your face that proclaims "leper" to everyone you meet.

Perhaps you feel as though everyone knows what has been happening in your life. Perhaps you feel as though everyone is judging you as unclean and therefore they avoid you. I admit that the church can be a cold and uninviting place. We can find Pharisees and judgmental people there. We need to beware of seeking the approval of men over that of God. The fact remains that we have been fully accepted in Christ!

And there are others that need you. Others need to see what you see. Others need to see that the guaranteed health and wealth view of Christianity is a sham. Others need to see that God can be honored, Jesus can be exalted, and people can still love in the midst of horrible, agonizing pain. Others in the church need the gifts God has given you for their good and His glory. Perhaps you can serve or teach or encourage. Perhaps you can contribute, lead, or show mercy. (Romans 12:7–8)

And you need to experience God's presence in Word and sacrament. One of Jesus' last prayers for you and me in the Garden of Gethsemane was for the Father to sanctify us by the Word of Truth. It is God's Word that saved us and it is God's Word that sustains us. We have seen already how our feelings are fickle, how our hearts are faint, and how our minds are weak. Dietrich Bonhoeffer, the Lutheran pastor killed in a Nazis concentration camp, said it is easier for us to believe the Word from the mouth of a brother or sister than it is to believe it from our own lips. And Luther cautioned, "The devil is a greater rascal than you think he is. You do not yet know what sort of fellow he is and what a desperate rogue you are. His definite design is to get you tired of the Word and in this way draw you away from it."

I hope you find what I found when I was tempted to flee from the community of faith. Rather than being distant and removed, I found myself closer to others than I had ever experienced before on earth. Real relationships come from risking and reaching out. I have been blessed with Spirit-filled pastors and friends. Rather than being shocked or alarmed by my confessions, they responded with grace and acceptance and mercy. The fellowship of the forgiven is rich and intimate. It is so sad that many don't taste this.

It surprises me not at all that satan is trying to keep you from your only Hope. He doesn't want the truth to get through. Luther knew this full well: "Although you have wicked thoughts, you should not despair because of them; only see to it that they do not take you captive...You must learn that if you are a Christian, you will without a doubt experience all kinds of opposition and evil inclinations in the flesh. For when you have faith, there will be a hundred more evil thoughts and a hundred more temptations than before."

You are under attack, dear Christian friend. Let the battle belong to the Lord. Call upon Him and He will deliver you. Ask Him to fight it for you. Seek His nourishment as given at His supper. Seek His transforming work in His Word. Seek His presence in prayer. Seek His fellowship with His people. Bathe your wounds in His forgiveness. And do this all the more as your feelings tell you otherwise.

Your brother who has been where you are,

Craig

P.S.

"For where two or three come together in my name, there am I with them." (Matthew 18:20)

"Let us hold unswervingly to the hope we profess, for he who promised is faithful ... Let us not give up meeting together, as some are in the habit of doing, but let us encourage one another—and all the more as you see the Day approaching." (Hebrews 10:23, 25)

"Jesus answered, 'It is written: 'Man does not live on bread alone, but on every word that comes from the mouth of God.''" (Matthew 4:4)

"The Lord Jesus, on the night he was betrayed, took bread, and when he had given thanks, he broke it and said, 'This is my body, which is for you; do this in remembrance of me.' In the same way, after supper he took the cup, saying 'This cup is the new covenant in my blood; do this, whenever you drink it, in remembrance of me.' For whenever you eat this bread and drink this cup, you proclaim the Lord's death until he comes." (I Corinthians 11:23–26)

Chapter 11 Questions for Reflection and/or Discussion:

1. What activities in your average day do you do even though you don't always feel like doing them?

2. What would be the consequences (to yourself and to others) if you didn't do those activities listed in question one?

3. What God-given gifts can you offer to others at your congregation?

4. What time of day is best for you to carve out ten or more minutes to be alone with the Lord?

Letter Twelve

I don't feel God's love; I feel so alone!

Dear Michelle,
It would not surprise me if this were one of the loneliest times you have experienced on earth. When we find ourselves in the crucible, being ground down, the rest of the world—and God—seem so distant and uncaring. It seems as if everyone else is happy and carefree. It is very common to feel the way you are feeling. And to make matters worse, I suspect your present desire is to distance yourself even farther from others and from Him. If you stop and think about it, however, you will realize that this would be a mistake. After all, God Himself said, "It is not good for man to be alone." (Gen. 2:18)

We were made to be in relationship, both with God and with others. When we remove ourselves from community, we must find some counterfeit to fill the void. This is where the various addictions come into play. Some people turn to alcohol or drugs or sex. Some turn to work or exercise or recreation. Some read; some eat. Whatever becomes our master is relentless and offers a heavy yoke and an insatiable thirst. Such a choice will prove costly in the long run.

But you might be protesting, "But I have tried reaching out to others; no one seems interested. Everyone is in their own little world." Sadly, that might be true with the circle of people that you know. I rarely come across many people today who see their world as anything other than busy and hectic. If you do find someone with time on their hands, chances are they won't understand you or your present trials. "A friend loves at all times, but a brother is born for adversity." (Prov. 17:17) Companionship is such a great and gracious gift from God and right now you are desperately seeking it. I think you have a glimpse of what Jesus must have experienced on the cross when He felt abandoned by friends and even His heavenly Father.

I am amazed when I study the last few days and hours of our Lord's life. Check for yourself in John chapters 13–20. If it were I, I can envision much grumbling and complaining and not a little protesting over the bogus charges leveled against me. Not Jesus. His thoughts are toward His Father (staying up all night praying in the garden). They are with his friends, assuring them that He will prepare a room for them, send a Comforter, and return for them some day. They are for the providing of His mother. They are with the guilty crowd mocking Him as He forgives them for they don't know what they are doing. To the end, despite being blatantly rejected, physically abused, completely exhausted, and emotionally ridiculed, Jesus continues to give.

We servants are no greater than our Master. It might possibly be that those near you, perhaps friends or family, have deserted you. Like Job's fair-weather friends, maybe someone has devalued your trial by giving you quick and easy advice. Maybe, in their effort to avoid getting too close to your uncomfortable pain, they tried applying a soggy band-aid to the titanic-sized hole in your heart. Whatever the case, the result is that no one listens, no one weeps with you, no one wrestles with you. They all run away for fear you might be contagious.

The good news is that, while you might feel lonely, the fact remains—you are not alone. The faith that saves you and me is attached to a living, breathing Person. And He has given us some of the most precious promises in all of Scripture. "And surely I am with you always, to the very end of the age." (Mt. 28:20) "Never will I leave you; never will I forsake you." (Heb. 13:5) "When you pass through the waters, I will be with you; and when you pass through the rivers, they will not sweep over you. When you walk through the fire, you will not be burned ... Since you are precious and honored in my sight, and because I love you." (Is. 43:2, 4) "Listen to me ... you whom I have upheld since you were conceived, and have carried you since your birth. Even to your old age and gray hairs I am he, and I am he who will sustain you. I have made you and I will carry you; I will sustain you and I will rescue you." (Is. 46:3–4) When these facts slowly sink in, we will realize that since we can't control circumstances or others down here, we are free to trust God and love others. This puts a whole new perspective on our problems and life.

Rather than focusing on getting (or what we are NOT getting), our new vision looks for opportunities to give. Rather than waiting to first receive from another, we boldly and unconditionally initiate and offer the very things we want for ourselves. New questions preoccupy our minds: What can I give in this circumstance? What do I want to be? What would glorify God here? Even our prayers begin to change. We start uttering, "God, use me today. Love people through me." And it starts to happen. It need not be any great cause or huge program. It might be how we converse with the next person we speak with, focusing on what they need, exploring how we might feel and react in their shoes. Suddenly we realize that we are relating to others and not trying to fix them or use them to fix us. We also realize that "we no longer live, but Christ lives within us." (Gal. 2:20)

And one day we wake up and it dawns on us. Our schedule for the day is filled. We have places to go and people to see. We feel purposeful instead of just needy. We know our lives have meaning because God is using us to touch others. We feel intensely alive. Pain and joy both take on greater clarity. We actually begin to weep with those who weep and rejoice with those who rejoice. We feel and admit our own pain more vividly and quickly. It still stings to have another overlook us but we understand how their flesh, like ours, can be preoccupied in the midst of pain. And we might see that our friendships are now deeper than ever before. We also might find ourselves gravitating toward those who have walked through high waters and fiery coals. And lo and behold, joy has come in the morning! Tears might well up quicker than ever before but so do belly laughs.

It is more blessed to give than to receive and, believe it or not, because you are enduring the present trial, you will have more to offer to others in the future.

Walking with you,

Craig

P.S.

"Cursed is the one who trusts in man, who depends upon flesh for his strength and whose heart turns away from the Lord. He will be like a bush in the wastelands; he will not see prosperity when it comes. He will dwell in the parched places of the desert, in a salt land where no one lives. But blessed is the man who trusts in the Lord, whose confidence is in him. He will be like a tree planted by the water that sends out its roots by the stream. It does not fear when heat comes; its leaves are always green. It has no worries in a year of drought and never fails to bear fruit." (Jeremiah 17:5–8)

"Praise be to the God and Father of our Lord Jesus Christ, the Father of compassion and the God of all comfort, who comforts us in all our troubles, so that we can comfort those in any trouble with the comfort we ourselves have received from God." (II Corinthians 1:3–4)

"Can a mother forget the baby at her breast and have no compassion on the child she has borne? Though she may forget, I will not forget you! See, I have engraved you on the palms of my hands." (Isaiah 49:15–16)

Chapter 12 Questions for Reflection and/or Discussion:

1. What do you do when you feel lonely?

2. Who is currently your best friend? How do they help you best?

3. To whom and how could you reach out to others?

4. How might your present ordeal prepare you to give to others now and in the future?

Letter Thirteen

Why did God allow evil to happen? Will this junk happen in heaven?

Dear Michelle,
I sure hope and pray that my words in former letters have been helpful to you. You are wrestling with some of life's most challenging questions. Theologians have argued over the problem of evil for centuries. I am more than a little nervous as I venture some kind of answer for you today!

Your question reminds me of one of the last conversations I had with my dear aunt before she succumbed to bone marrow cancer. I had just delivered some ice cream one warm afternoon to her and we were sitting on her patio. Since I was her nephew who happened to teach Bible to high school seniors, she felt free to ask me some spiritual questions from time to time. This was not part of normal conversation, mind you, in my family. As I squirmed in my lounge chair, I knew we were headed to depths never before approached.

The agony and horror of inevitable death by cancer had led my aunt to think about many things. Pain and death have a way of waking us up and forcing us to consider issues about God and life and the next life that the day-to-day trappings down here anesthetize us to. I was privileged to be walking on this holy ground with her and now God had placed me in that chair across from my inquiring aunt. My ice cream started to melt faster!

I began by sharing what I had heard and read. C.S. Lewis talks about God's giving Adam and Eve free will in the garden. (*Mere Christianity*) God didn't want to make robots but wanted a loving relationship. In order to have true love, there must be a choice. As those words came out in that setting, however, I felt they were incomplete.

Others have maintained that the problem of evil will always remain a mystery. What is important for us to know is what God has chosen to do about it. In a nutshell, that was to send Jesus as atonement for Adam's disobedience and to provide the way for us to one day go where there is no more pain and suffering. Judging from my aunt's expression, I think that was more comforting. Fortunately, our pastor had several conversations with my aunt and I hope he covered for my awkward and clumsy efforts.

I do know this. Before the world began, God had planned to show His love for us by sending His Son. He also had you in mind then. Ephesians says as much, "For he chose us in him before the creation of the world to be holy and blameless in his sight. In love he predestined us to be adopted as his sons through Jesus Christ." (Eph. 1:4–5) God's ultimate plan has been, is, and will be Jesus. "He is the image of the invisible God, the firstborn over all creation. For by him all things were created: things in heaven and on earth, visible and invisible, whether thrones or powers or rulers or authorities; all things were created by him and for him. He is before all things, and in him all things hold together … For God was pleased to have all his fullness dwell in him, and through him to reconcile to himself all things, whether things on earth or things in heaven, by making peace through his blood, shed on the cross." (Col. 1:15–17, 19–20)

When I was younger, I used to think that sending Jesus was Plan B after Plan A had failed. That view is incorrect. Luther puts it more boldly still. He maintains that when we get to heaven and discover the sweet and awesome glory of God, we will see that this plan was more than worth it. Luther says we will be willing to go through it all again for His glory.

And it is on that point that year after year students have asked me, "Will we be able to sin in heaven?"

God is making a new heaven and a new earth. He is preparing a place for us. (Jn. 14:2) We will have new and glorified bodies. (I Cor. 15:52–53) The good work He began in us, restoring us to His image and conforming us to the likeness of Christ, will be finished. (Phil. 1:6) Satan and all evil will be bound forever in the lake of burning fire. There, "they will be tormented day and night forever and ever." (Rev. 20:10)

And what about heaven? "Nothing impure will ever enter it, nor will anyone who does what is shameful or deceitful, but only those whose names are written in the Lamb's book of life." (Rev. 21:27) Note well the words "nothing impure will EVER enter it." The Lord will say to the devil and his angels, "Depart from me, you who are cursed, into the eternal fire prepared for you." (Mt. 25:41)

Think about it. No more temptation. No more conflicting tensions and thoughts. No more internal war between the flesh and the spirit. Only a perfect union of our will and God's will. At last, we will enjoy perfect unity with God and with others. True love will flourish. Listen to some of the most beautiful, hopeful words in Scripture: "And I heard a loud voice from the throne saying, 'Now the dwelling of God is with men, and he will live with them. They will be his people, and God himself will be with them and be their God. He will wipe every tear from their eyes. There will be no more death or mourning or crying or pain, for the old order of things has passed away." (Rev. 21:3–4)

Do you know what God says about people who have such hope, who dream such a big dream, who long for such a better world? "He is not ashamed to be called their God, for he has prepared a city for them." (Heb. 11:16)

To all this, I can think of only one more thing to say. I didn't start praying for this myself until I had tasted the depth of my sin and the piercing pain that can be part of this world. Appropriately, it is how God's Word ends in Revelation:

"Amen. Come, Lord Jesus." (Rev. 22:20)

Waiting more eagerly for that day than ever before,

Craig

P.S.

"He who testifies to these things says, 'Yes, I am coming soon.'" (Rev. 22:20)

"Behold, I will create new heavens and a new earth. The former things will not be remembered, nor will they come to mind. But be glad and rejoice forever in what I will create, for I will create Jerusalem to be a delight and its people a joy. I will rejoice over Jerusalem and take delight in my people; the sound of weeping and of crying will be heard in it no more." (Isaiah 65:17–19)

"'Never again will there be in it an infant who lives but a few days, or an old man who does not live out his years…They will not toil in vain or bear children doomed to misfortune; for they will be a people blessed by the Lord … They will neither harm nor destroy on all my holy mountain,' says the Lord.'" (Isaiah 65:20, 23, 25)

Chapter 13 Questions for Reflection and/or Discussion:

1. Some people have trouble picturing heaven. I find it helpful to focus on what will not be there. List earthly trials that will be nonexistent in heaven.

2. Dream of what your life will be like without your sinful flesh in heaven. (Think of thoughts, words, and actions.)

3. I maintain there is a more wonderful and fascinating question behind the problem of evil: why would God send His one and only Son to die for the whole world and us? Think about it.

4. For what questions in your life might you never find answers?

What does it all mean?

Dear Michelle,
We have come full circle. As chapter one ended, we were reminded of Romans 11:33—"How unsearchable his judgments, and his paths beyond tracing out!" It would be presumptuous and not a little arrogant for me to sit here and claim to know precisely what God is doing in your life through these trials. But the aim of these letters, indeed my fervent prayer, has been to lead you to our Hope.

From my own experience, from that of countless friends, and especially from the records of the ancient witnesses, I am convinced that God is doing something in you right now. I am convinced that He is giving you microscopic attention, as a surgeon might a patient during surgery. I am convinced that you have been called to a holy place, a place where you have a distinct opportunity to know God as few people do on this earth.

There is a Bigger Story going on behind all our smaller ones. (*Sacred Romance*) Whatever is happening to you on the surface, there is something deeper rumbling underneath. It isn't about your poor health or your failing relationship. It isn't about your financial condition or your job security. It is about the two main characters in your life story: you and Him. What is He showing you about Him, about life, about you, about you and Him? What is He doing in you? I know it is painfully obvious what He is NOT doing with your circumstances, so look deeper. You matter more to Him. How is your character being developed? How is your mind being transformed?

Augustine observed that the whole of the Christian life is a holy longing. What do you long for? Do you long for a world with no tears? Do you long to be a more loving person? Do you long to be surrounded by people who know you and love you just because you are you? Do you long to be free from pain and suffering? Do you long to be free of fear and guilt? Do you long to see God face to face? The day is coming, you know, when all these longings will be met. But it isn't here. Not yet.

Whatever is happening in your life right now, it is a transient blip on the eternal radar screen. There will come a day when it will be forgotten (Isaiah 65:17) (Perhaps there will even be days on earth where you don't think about it much too!) Luther put it all into perspective: "It would be a great error to estimate God's goodness and grace only by your lot here on earth … The true, supreme, and best blessing is not temporal possessions but the eternal blessing that God has called us to His holy Gospel ... To him who properly appreciates this blessing everything else is trifle, even though he lacks temporal blessing, is poor, sick, despised, unfortunate, and burdened with all sorts of adversities. For he sees that he always keeps more than he has lost."

I like this image of sanctification. A man clenches his two fists tightly. His face is red and drops of sweat bead upon his forehead. Yet, one by one, his fingers are slowly, gently pried away from the objects of his obsession. Finally, he falls exhausted, head bowed, arms extended, and palms up. It is then that he begins to see all the blessings that God is pouring into his ready and available hands. Such is the picture of our walking through life down here. We gradually surrender the objects of our most earnest affection. The amazing thing is this: we are so frightened of losing what we cannot keep that we fail to see what we cannot lose. And that is what our heart deeply yearns for—Him and His unfailing love. He wants us to drop our playthings so we can embrace Him.

I am excited for you. No, I get no perverse, sadistic pleasure from another's pain. But I know the journey you are on. I have been there. And when I meet others who have also been there, in that dark night of the soul, I ask them this question: would you do it all over again to get where you are now, knowing God and yourself as you now do? Invariably, every person says without hesitation, with a reverent nod of the head, "Yes!" And this comes from an earthly perspective! Imagine what we will see from the angle of eternity!

Once more, let us sit at Luther's feet: "One Christian who has been tried is worth a hundred who have not been tried, for the blessing of God grows in trials. He who has experienced them can teach, comfort, and advise many in bodily and spiritual matters ... Oh! His grace and goodness toward us is so immeasurably great, that without great assaults and trials it cannot be understood."

"I pray that you, being rooted and established in love, may have power, together with all the saints, to grasp how wide and long and high and deep is the love of Christ, and to know this love that surpasses knowledge—that you may be filled to the measure of all the fullness of God. Now to him who is able to do immeasurably more than all we ask or imagine, according to his power that is at work within us, to him be glory in the church and in Christ Jesus throughout all generations, for ever and ever! Amen." (Eph. 3:17b–21)

Michelle, you are in good hands, because He is **for** the faint of heart!

Your fellow traveler cheering you onward and upward in Him,

Craig

P.S.

"We are hard pressed on every side, but not crushed; perplexed, but not in despair; persecuted, but not abandoned; struck down, but not destroyed. We always carry around in our body the death of

Jesus, so that the life of Jesus may also be revealed in our body." (II Corinthians 4:8–10)

"Therefore we do not lose heart. Though outwardly we are wasting away, yet inwardly we are being renewed day by day. For our light and momentary troubles are achieving for us an eternal glory that far outweighs them all. So we fix our eyes not on what is seen, but on what is unseen. For what is seen is temporary, but what is unseen is eternal." (II Corinthians 4:16–18)

"I consider everything a loss compared to the surpassing greatness of knowing Christ Jesus my Lord, for whose sake I have lost all things. I consider them rubbish, that I may gain Christ and be found in him ... I want to know Christ and the power of his resurrection." (Philippians 3:8, 10)

Chapter 14 Questions for Reflection and/or Discussion:

1. What do you deeply long for? (List several answers.)

2. What things or people has God pried out of your grasp?

3. What do you think Luther meant by his quote: "His grace and goodness toward us is so immeasurably great, that without great assaults and trials it cannot be understood"?

4. What might God be doing in your life right now?

Climb on these Shoulders
to Get a Better View

The Bible (especially Psalms 1, 4, 5, 6, 13, 23, 25, 27, 31,
32, 34, 38, 40, 42, 51, 55, 62, 63, 66, 69, 71, 77, 86, 103,
116, 118, 121, 138, 139, 142, 143, 145)

Allender, Dan Dr. (1990). *The Wounded Heart.* Colorado
Springs, CO: Navpress.

Crabb, Larry Dr. (1993). *Finding God.* Grand Rapids,
MI: Zondervan.

Crabb, Larry Dr. (2001). *Shattered Dreams.* Colorado
Springs, CO: WaterBrook Press.

Crabb, Larry Dr. (2002). *The Pressure's Off.* Colorado
Springs, CO: WaterBrook Press.

Curtis, Brent and Eldredge, John. (1997). *The Sacred
Romance.* Nashville, TN: Thomas Nelson Publishers.

Eldredge, John. (2000). *The Journey of Desire.* Nashville,
TN: Thomas Nelson Publishers.

Elliot, Elisabeth. (1990). *A Path Through Suffering.* Ann Arbor, MI: Servant Publications.

Kreeft, Peter. (1986). *Making Sense Out of Suffering.* Ann Arbor, MI: Servant Books.

Plass, Ewald M. (1959). *What Luther Says: An Anthology.* St. Louis, MO: Concordia Publishing House.

Yancey, Phillip. (1997). *Disappointment With God.* Grand Rapids, MI: Zondervan Publishing House.

If You Question
God's Love for You....

You are the apple of His eye.

(Ps. 17:8)

You are engraved on the palm of His hand.

(Is. 49:16)

He has counted the hairs on your head.

(Mt. 10:29–31)

You are His offspring.

(Acts 17:28)

He chose you before creation.

(Eph. 1:11–12)

He made you fearfully and wonderfully.

(Ps. 139:14)

He knit you together in your mother's womb.

(Ps. 139:13)

He has been with you and will be till the day you die.

(Is. 46:3–4)

He lavishes great love on you.

(I Jn. 3:1)

He calls you His child.

(I Jn. 3:1)

He gives you all your good gifts.

(James 1:17)

He will graciously give you all you need.

(Phil. 4:19)

He is for you and not against you.

(Rom. 8:31)

He works for your good in all things.

(Rom. 8:28)

He has prepared good works for you to do.

(Eph. 2:10)

You are His workmanship.

(Eph. 2:10)

He will complete the good work He began in you.

(Phil. 1:6)

He is the author and perfecter of your faith.

(Heb. 12:2)

He takes great delight in you.

(Zeph. 3:17)

He rejoices over you with singing.

(Zeph. 3:17)

He speaks in your defense.

(I Jn. 2:1)

He does not condemn you.

(Rom. 8:1)

He is the source of all your comfort.

(II Cor. 1:3–4)

He is close to you when you are brokenhearted.

(Ps. 34:18)

He carries you close to His heart.

(Is. 40:11)

He will wipe every tear from your eye.

(Rev. 21:4)

He will sustain you and carry you and rescue you.

(Is. 46:4)

He will give your soul the richest of fare.

(Is. 55:2)

He turns your darkness into light.

(Ps. 8:18)

He is renewing you inwardly day by day.

(II Cor. 4:16)

He forgives you and cleanses you from all unrighteousness.

(I Jn. 1:9)

He does not treat you as your sins deserve.

(Ps. 103:10)

He has made you complete in Him.

(Col. 2:10)

He has made you holy in His sight, without blemish and free from accusation.

(Col. 1:22)

He has given you His righteousness.

(Rom. 5:19)

He will make you stand firm, come what may, till the end.

(II Cor. 1:21)

He is your life.

(Col. 3:3)

He has seated you next to Him in heaven.

(Eph. 2:6–7)

He is removing your idolatries and impurities from you.

(Ezek. 36:25)

He is transforming you from one degree of glory into the next.

(II Cor. 3:18)

He lives in you.

(Gal. 2:20)

He bears fruit through you.

(Jn. 15:5)

He will never leave you or forsake you.

(Heb. 13:5)

He died for you.

(Rom. 5:8)

What others have said about FOR THE FAINT OF HEART:

❧❀❦

"If you have ever at painful times questioned your faith or your Lord, this piece is for you. The real source of hope and help is the Word, and this work provides it. I could not put it down."

—Mr. Ron Brandhorst,
Teacher and Adult Bible Study Leader,
Denver Lutheran High School

"Craig Parrott offers a catalogue of comfort for hurting Christians as he draws on the wisdom of Scripture, Luther, and a variety of respected counselors. His transparency in sharing his own struggles, and those of the students he counsels, enables him to speak with a certainty that comes only with life experience as well as study. He deals with the difficult questions and brings the reader to have hope in the promises of God in Jesus Christ for time and eternity. I would recommend the book for all that are in need of that hope."

—Rev. Dwight Hellmers,
Pastor, St. Luke's Lutheran Church,
Golden, Colorado

Craig Parrott, M.S., M.A.

Craig Parrott has taught Bible and English in Lutheran High Schools for over twenty-four years. Having a master's degree in professional writing, he has written numerous articles for THE CALEB COMMENT and LUTHERAN EDUCATION, quarterly publications for Christian educators. He has experienced divorce both as a child and as an adult, witnessed his aunt battle bone marrow cancer, and grieved over his father's death. From leading retreats, workshops, and seminars to facilitating loss support groups, Craig has walked with hundreds of youth and adults through their trials and tribulations.

Printed in the United States
200033BV00002B/253-1026/A